**By Jane West**

Cartoons:
Phil Hailstone

Published by:

**Teachers' Pocketbooks**
Laurel House, Station Approach,
Alresford, Hampshire
SO24 9JH, UK
Tel: +44 (0)1962 735573
Fax: +44 (0)1962 733637
E-mail:
sales@teacherspocketbooks.co.uk
Website:
www.teacherspocketbooks.co.uk

*Teachers' Pocketbooks is an imprint
of Management Pocketbooks Ltd.*

Series Consultant: **Brin Best**.

This edition published 2004.

ISBN 1 903776 60 0

British Library Cataloguing-in-Publication Data – A catalogue
record for this book is available from the British Library.

Design, typesetting and graphics by Efex Ltd. Printed in UK.

# Contents

# How to use this pocketbook

This book is a resource to support all teachers involved in organising school trips. It contains practical advice and information which will be useful for headteachers, governors, senior management, educational visits co-ordinators (EVCs), teachers, teaching assistants, parents, volunteer supervisors and may be particularly valuable for the first-time trip organiser.

It can be used in several ways:

- To help you **plan** better visits
- To help you **evaluate** whether a trip has met your **educational objectives**
- To **inform** and **remind** those who are unclear about their rights and responsibilities when organising trips
- To answer relevant questions and **avoid common pitfalls**

# How to use this pocketbook

- To **reflect** – why do the same trip every year? Why not re-evaluate your school visits and try out some different ideas?
- To **train** – you can use this booklet to help train new colleagues to organise school trips
- To **reassure** staff who are nervous or unsure about organising trips
- To **read selectively**. Read it cover to cover or dip into sections – it's up to you

# How to use this pocketbook

## Health warning

School trips can be great fun for you and your students, but they are potentially hazardous. Details about rules and regulations, health and safety, first aid, the law and so on were correct at time of going to press, **but always check that your information is up-to-date.**

If you follow news in the press about school trips it may be hard to believe that accidents are rare but *'the overwhelming majority take place without any cause for concern whatsoever'* (general secretary of NAHT).

Unfortunately, as a nation we are becoming increasingly litigious and parents may look for someone to blame if something goes wrong. A clear audit trail for planning, risk assessment and safety management issues, together with information about who is responsible for what and when, is essential.

Getting Started

 General Tips for Successful Trips

 Trips for Culture and Commerce

 Outdoor and Activity Trips

 Overseas and Exchange Trips

 Health and Safety

 School Trips and the Law

 Further Information

# Getting Started

# So you're organising a school trip?

Congratulations! Educational visits and trips can be some of the most rewarding aspects of teaching. They give you a chance to get to know your students in a completely different environment and to develop your working relationship as a teacher and mentor. Students, meanwhile, are given the opportunity to enjoy educational experiences outside the classroom and to practise team-building skills.

Your students will begin to see you as a human being with interests and enthusiasms, and not just their teacher. Although they may not admit it, students will appreciate the fact that you've taken the time and trouble to organise a trip for them – an educational reward for you and your students.

This pocketbook is full of practical tips to help you plan a successful and memorable trip.

# The role of the EVC

Your school will probably have a senior member of staff who has been appointed Educational Visits Co-ordinator. Maintained schools **should** appoint an EVC but it is good practice for all schools. EVCs receive special training, usually from the LEA.

The EVC should always be an experienced senior member of staff as the role carries great responsibility. In smaller schools (or where no EVC has been appointed) the role of the EVC will default to the Head.

When you start organising your trip the EVC will be a wonderful resource and will be able to advise you about the paperwork involved!

# How the EVC can help you

Although the EVC is an important resource, it is not their job to plan the trip for you. EVCs **are** responsible for:

- Developing a school policy with clear procedures that follow guidelines – including a plan for managing a serious problem and administering medication (made available to all trip organisers)
- Checking that visits meet your LEA's requirements/risk assessment
- Assigning competent people to lead or supervise a visit
- Organising training for leaders and other adults going on a visit
- Checking CRB (criminal records bureau) disclosures and qualifications/experience of staff leading the trip or activity
- Providing full information for parents and checking consent forms are signed
- Organising emergency arrangements, checking medical needs are met and first aid is available
- Keeping records, reviewing systems and monitoring practice

If your school has not appointed an EVC, responsibility defaults to your headteacher.

# The role of the LEA or employer

If you work in a maintained school, the LEA is your employer and has responsibility for the health and safety of students on off-site visits. (The governing body is the employer in CTCs, voluntary-aided and non-maintained schools; the owner, governors or trustees are the employer in independent schools.) This is usually delegated to an individual within the school – the EVC – but the LEA retains the ultimate responsibility. The LEA/employer's role is to:

- Provide written guidelines
- Assess proposals for certain types of trips: residential, overseas visits or hazardous activities
- Provide emergency phone contact/access to named staff for advice
- Ensure training needs have been addressed
- Maintain appropriate insurance cover
- Establish procedures to monitor and review safety

# The role of the Outdoor Education Adviser

Many LEAs have an Outdoor Education Adviser (OEA) – a very useful contact and source of information. This is the person at the LEA who will ultimately approve your trip. It is their job to ensure EVCs are:

- Appropriately trained
- Competent
- Monitored

The LEA should also provide written guidelines for governors, headteachers and staff, including advice on risk assessment and insurance cover. In addition they should supply emergency telephone contacts.

# Independent schools

DfES guidance says that in independent schools responsibility for health and safety lies with governing bodies (also in foundation and voluntary-aided schools).

The LEA Outdoor Education Advisers' Panel provides training for all newly appointed EVCs in maintained schools. Supported by the DfES Pupil Safety Unit, this training, jointly organised by the Independent Schools Adventure Activities Association (ISAAA) and the Royal Geographical Society, is now available to independent schools.

A one-day course costs about £150 and covers:

- Roles and responsibilities
- Risk assessment/risk management
- Leadership, competence and supervision
- Information and advice for the EVC

# Parents and governors

Parents have a 'reasonable expectation' that the planned trip is approved.

The governing body, through the SMT, needs to check that the school policy will ensure that trips are planned effectively and safely – you should inform them well in advance for less routine visits. The EVC should draft the policy and check any amendments from the SMT or governors.

Governors, who are likely to be accountable in law, must be satisfied that your risk assessment has been carried out properly (see pages 86-92) and that any training needs have been addressed.  They should:

- Ensure trips have stated objectives
- Ensure plans comply with regulations – you or your Head will need to report back to them after a trip
- Assess plans for overnight stays and non-UK travel

# DfES Guidelines

EVCs should receive specific training (first aid, minibus driving and life-saving), as well as support and on-going information from the OEA.

Through your EVC, **the LEA has to approve all residential, overseas visits or hazardous activities.** Proposals and risk assessments must be submitted to the LEA a minimum of eight weeks before the proposed trip.

Your EVC will have this useful publication and its three supplements – *1998 Health and Safety of Pupils on Educational Visits (HASPEV)*:

- *Standards for LEAs in overseeing educational visits*
- *Health and safety – responsibilities and powers*
- *Standards for leading adventure activities – a handbook for group leaders*

Phone 0845 6022260 (Ref HSPV2) for a free copy, or download it from www.dfes.gov.uk.

# Training for trip leaders

Even if you've led dozens of trips, there's always something new to learn. Tragedies, although rare, have resulted in new government guidelines – ask your EVC for the current information.

If you're planning your first trip, your EVC should ensure that you receive training in the following areas:

### Purpose – cost – outcome

Why has this trip been organised? What (on-going) benefits does it offer to students? How much will it cost? Are the proposed outcomes realistic?

Remember, all trips have to be justified to the LEA (maintained schools), your headteacher and to students' parents/carers (all schools).

### Monitoring and evaluation

What quality controls are in place to ensure that the trip is a valuable experience for students and value for money? How will the trip be evaluated?

# Training for trip leaders

### Budgeting

Writing a budget for trips and where to go for the best deals. (Your colleagues will share their knowledge with you too.)

### Emergency procedures

Trip leaders should be **qualified first aiders** and have taken a course in **driving minibuses**.

Health and Safety regulations should be explained alongside how to conduct a comprehensive **risk assessment**.

What emergency procedures does the school operate? Trip leaders should be given a **manual** that includes numbers for emergency services, and mobile numbers for the headteacher and senior staff. The manual should include a **media policy** so you know what to do if you have to deal with the Press.

# Educational trip or holiday?

Educational trips are those which are part of the National Curriculum or are helpful in broadening it or enriching children's educational experience.

Trips such as skiing trips may offer a great experience, but are just a holiday.

The lines become blurred if, for example, as a PE teacher you want to take your team on a playing tour abroad. While this would undoubtedly be a great experience for your pupils, it could be costly. It's a good idea to discuss this with parents first. Avoid the scenario where an excited pupil goes home to tell a parent that the team is going to South Africa – and then the parent finds out they have to find an additional £600 for this unplanned holiday.

If parents are willing to pay or raise the money, give them as much time as possible – up to two terms is reasonable for a costly trip.

# First (general) checklist

Checklists will be different for each trip or activity. Prepare checklists for what you need to do before, during and even after the visit. It's a good idea to start with general information such as:

- Who is responsible for leading the trip? (Always appoint a deputy, too)
- What is the size of the group and, therefore, how many staff/adult supervisors are required? (See page 106)
- Age of students
- Do any students have special needs?
- What is the general level of ability required?
- What emergency procedures are in place?

Once you have completed your general list, you can go on to prepare a detailed checklist for individual trips (see eg on p33).

# What if some students can't afford the trip?

Even a few pounds may be beyond the means of some students, so be sensitive when organising trips and check your school policy on this.

### Government guidelines

- Any trip that takes place mainly in school time is subject to legislation – **the determining factor for participation must not be ability to pay**. LEAs and schools must make their charging policy available to parents. When requesting money, explain whether payment is for a specific activity or a general contribution. You must be clear whether or not contributions are voluntary

- Notionally, visits in school time (including transport) should be free of charge, but schools can ask for 'voluntary donations'. Parents who are unable or unwilling to contribute may not be discriminated against

- Overseas trips are usually offered out of school time and are not subject to the same legislation

# When pupils can't afford the trip

If you plan to organise lots of trips for your classes, you will need to think carefully about how to include students whose parents/carers can't afford 'extras'.

Schools can only ask for 'voluntary donations' for trips planned during the school day. Your EVC will tell you if this is a policy in your school.

Your school may be eligible for government grants to fund school trips. To qualify, more than 35% of students must claim free school meals. Remember, schools should offer a range of visits both in and out of school time; otherwise you may risk grievances from parents.

Parents who receive benefits can recover the cost of out-of-hours trips and of residential trips that take place mostly or partly during school if they are **a necessary part of the curriculum**.

# Raising money for a trip

When you ask parents to contribute towards a trip it's important that you clarify whether they're paying for a trip or for general funds towards the school. If you take this approach, *you must tell parents what proportion of the money is specific/general and parents should be allowed to opt out if they wish*. For example, the theatre trip costs £15, but you ask for an additional £2.50 for general school funds. **If the trip is an optional extra, you cannot charge parents a subsidy**.

If there is a shortfall for pupils whose parents cannot pay, you will need to raise funds to cover this. By law, you cannot discriminate against these pupils. If you can't raise the additional funds, the trip must be cancelled.

There are lots of ways to raise small amounts of money: cake sales, raffles, car boot sales, quiz nights, out-of-uniform day, PTA events, alumni giving. To raise a large amount of money consider developing a fundraising team/plan. (See page 126 for useful websites.)

**NB** If there is surplus money at the end of a trip, agree in advance whether the school will keep this or whether it will be returned to parents.

# Keeping track of the money

We've all read cases of teachers charged with serious professional misconduct or facing criminal charges because they've made a mess of the trip finances. It's unlikely that you will be dealing directly with the money, but it's a good idea to liaise with the person who is. This is usually the school secretary or the bursar.

# Managing the money

It's then a question of following a few simple rules:

- The **deposit** should be 10% of the total cost. If a third party is organising your trip it may be non-refundable. Make sure parents/carers are aware of this
- If there are to be **staged payments**, set clear deadlines and allow plenty of time to chase up late payers!
- Where possible, set up a **separate bank account** for trips
- **Discourage cash payments**. It's much easier to keep track of cheques or postal orders. Record the date the payment was received and if given cash, write a receipt
- Ideally **one designated person** should receive payments. A colleague who forgets that 'Saffy' gave them a cheque can cause serious headaches
- Ensure that as trip leader you have access to **emergency cash** and a credit card with at least £5,000 available (more for overseas trips)

# General Tips for
# Successful Trips

# Like a military operation – pre-planning

Taking students out of school needs to be carefully planned; being prepared will give you the confidence to deal with any surprises.

- Use online resources, guides, maps, leaflets and tourist information materials
- If possible, visit the site beforehand. Otherwise, take advice from someone who's been there, eg another school (or LEA) in the area
- If you're booking a coach, ask the provider for their advice. They will have done this many times before and will also have done their own risk assessment
- Even if you know the area well, take an A-Z map with you. It may come in handy!

# Like a military operation – pre-planning

- Establish a rendezvous point in case anyone becomes separated from the group
- Prepare checklists for what you need to do before and during the visit
- Decide whether you want to give out worksheets before the trip or on the day
- If you have disabled students, check in advance that special needs can be met
- Discuss expected behaviour with students. Plan what to do if you need to send a child home
- Have a contingency plan in case your return is delayed

# Volunteer helpers

Having parent helpers is a great way to get to know them better. Take time to explain to them the aims of the day and what you expect from them. Find out whether they have any first aid experience and tell them what to do in the case of accidents or illness. Make sure they are given:

- Copies of any worksheets
- A timetable of the day
- Contact details – get their mobile numbers and give yours
- A list of students for whom they are responsible and details of their special needs

Discuss any possible problems or potential dangers: traffic, machinery, tide-times, poisonous plants, dangerous animals, pickpockets and so on.

Volunteers who have not had a CRB check should not be left in sole charge of students, unless this is part of your risk assessment, and all volunteers should avoid being alone with a pupil.

# Arriving at your visit site

Your students (and you) will be judged on how they behave when they arrive at the visit site. Particularly if students are in uniform, it will be the school's reputation which is affected. *Before the visit* discuss and agree a code of behaviour with students:

- Explain what they should do/where they should go as soon as they arrive/get off the coach/train/plane
- Remind students who their group supervisor is – students should exit in small groups with their supervisor and re-group at a prearranged location
- Encourage students to be polite and considerate to other site users
- Ask students to turn off mobile phones – except for the designated person within a group
- Draw attention to how 'bunching' together on the pavement causes an obstruction
- Remind students they should not interrupt, distract or annoy other site users

# During the visit

Allow more time than you think you'll need for each stage of the day. Better to have students waiting around for a few minutes than to miss a connection or start time.

- Go through your checklist (page 33) before students leave the school grounds: equipment, food, tickets, passport, medication, worksheets, and so on
- Plan frequent toilet stops – check if you have to pay (eg at train stations)
- Prepare a number of quick quizzes for any 'waiting' periods, eg 'I-Spy'; *'Tell me three facts about the place we are going to visit/have just visited'; 'What year was this built/made?'* and so on
- If students are to split into groups, name the leader (or an appropriate adult), make sure that one of them has a mobile phone and that you have their number. You may prefer to use a 'school' mobile rather than give out your own number
- Encourage students to record the visit: to sketch, collect leaflets/bus tickets/postcards, photograph (disposable cameras), tape (dictaphones), video

# After the visit

Students will get most out of a visit when it is in context with other work they are already doing, so plan follow-up or extension work. For example:

- Scrap books, audio-visual records, or CDs
- Maps of the route
- Powerpoint presentation to other students/parents
- A guidebook for a younger class/disabled person making the same visit

Don't forget that you or your headteacher will need to report back to the governors about the trip – usually with 14 days of your return.

# Working with education officers

Most historic monuments, galleries and museums have education officers, and increasingly companies, too, have a member of staff responsible for schools. Give them as much notice as possible of your visit, and let them know your itinerary and details of any special needs/food requirements etc.

- Use their expertise/advice and discuss any on-site lectures or workshops, making sure they are suitable for your students. Education officers can often tailor workshops to specific requirements
- Discuss ideas for work to do before the visit and for follow-up/extension work
- Where resource packs are produced, look at these as early as possible. They may suggest ideas/information/resources you hadn't considered
- Check whether there are rules/discounts for groups

The requirement for galleries to 'attract more visitors from ethnic minorities and low-income families' means provision is changing and may differ from previous visits.

# Second (detailed) checklist

Your checklist will vary depending on the type of trip, but typically will include:

- Itinerary and worksheets
- List of students, staff and volunteer helpers
- Contact details within and outside school hours: parents, headteacher, governors, embassy, emergency services, travel operators (named person and contact no.)
- Equipment and named person with responsibility for it
- Health form (permission forms for each pupil): medication, allergies, long-standing problems – translate forms for EAL families
- Insurance, E111 forms, first aid kit
- Passports, driving licence, other documentation (tickets, vouchers, maps, guides)
- School credit card and emergency cash
- Food and water if necessary

# Notes

Getting Started

 General Tips for Successful Trips

 Trips for Culture and Commerce ◀

 Outdoor and Activity Trips

 Overseas and Exchange Trips

 Health and Safety

 School Trips and the Law

 Further Information

# Trips for Culture and Commerce

# Museums and galleries – awe and wonder

For some students, this may be the first time they have ever visited a museum or gallery and seen artefacts first hand. Seeing things on TV or in books is just not the same!

Try to encourage a sense of wonder: explain how the collection was developed and why. The use of primary sources in teaching can be a real eye-opener for pupils.

Many famous museums and galleries were first opened to the public in Victorian times as a way of educating poorer people and sharing the artefacts.

Often, interesting architecture is also a key part of the experience. For example, the Imperial War Museum in Manchester is dramatically different from conventional architecture based on right angles. The fragmented design aims to reflect the fragmenting consequences of war. And the Sainsbury Wing of the National Gallery in London aims to reproduce cathedral-like qualities and large scale to echo where the paintings would have been hung originally.

# Pre-planning for culture

Do try to avoid visits without context. Plan visits to museums and galleries to coincide with students' current work.

- Don't worry if you're not an expert – pre-planning will help, but look for the 'human' element: how/why something was made and for whom; what it meant to people at the time; how we interpret it now

- Today, we admire collections for artistic, historical, or scientific merit, but they also tell us about how people lived in the past. Help students to look for connections, contrasts and comparisons, and encourage them to explore their reactions to a particular painting or object

- Discuss rules or codes of behaviour such as why we can't touch artefacts

- Encourage students to be considerate towards other visitors and to turn off mobile phones

# First responses

It's OK not to 'get' a piece of art on first viewing. Before asking pupils for a response, give them time to explore the painting with their imaginations. You could suggest some possible starting points by asking questions such as:

- If the painting could speak, what would it say?
- What might the people in the painting say?
- Can you think of a piece of music that reminds you of this picture?
- Can you make up an alternative title for this picture?

There are no right or wrong answers; all responses are valid. Encourage pupils to make their own links with the outside world and to take control of their own learning.

# How to interpret 'art' – looking for clues

All artists are trying to communicate something, but it's not always obvious.
We need to look for clues. A modern audience will not necessarily interpret clues in the same way as the original audience. It helps to know the context of a painting: the artist's period in history, culture, patron, age, interests and so on.

**Biographical**    What do we know about the artist/subject? What can we guess from the main image/background/detail?

**Historical**    What do we know and what can we guess about the political and social history?
How might it be different if it were painted today or if it were a photograph or film?

# How to interpret 'art' – looking for clues

**Technical**      Does the painting/object belong to a particular 'school'?
How do we know?
What medium has been used?
(Watercolour/oil/engraving/pencil/ink/ceramic/textile/metal/marble)
Why do you think the artist might have worked in this size?
(Intimate art/impressive or public art/classical style?)
How has the artist demonstrated light and dark/
perspective/movement?

**Personal**      If you were going to 'interview' the artist/sitter, what questions
would you ask?

# But it's modern art – I think...

Until the twentieth century most western European art concentrated on story, symbol and form. JMW Turner was a notable exception with his studies of light and cloud.

But modern art can be completely different. People like Picasso subverted form and people like Mondrian (famous for painting geometric shapes) ignored almost everything that had gone before.

If you're not a fan of modern art, don't be put off by this or assume that students won't enjoy it. Even very young children can be astute in their appreciation of colour and form – they, too, paint in bright blocks of colour and can have an intuitive understanding of modern art.

Just ask the same questions you would of a classical painting:

* How does it make you feel? Why?
* What do you think the artist is trying to communicate?

# But I'm not an art expert...

Don't expect to have all the answers. Your students will probably see things you haven't considered. But looking for 'clues' will help students understand what the artist wanted to communicate.

- What are the most important parts of the picture? (Usually the largest or most prominent)
- Do you think the artist liked the object she/he was making? Why?
- Do you like it? Why? Why not?

The same sorts of questions can be used for looking at a variety of artefacts, buildings, heritage sites and so on.

# Heritage sites

The first time a child visits a heritage site can be an extraordinary experience – or it can be unutterably boring! Thoughtful planning will help ensure that your visit is enjoyable.

Heritage sites may not be quite what we expect. Some, like Stonehenge, are smaller than we imagine; some are much bigger and more exciting.

The key to a valuable experience is to help students understand something about the people who built the sites and lived there. Many sites now offer opportunities for students to 'become' archers from Agincourt, Victorian servants, soldiers from the Civil War, or guests at a Tudor banquet. Just having the chance to handle artefacts can give a sense of place and purpose. But do make sure that students understand what they can and can't touch – some artefacts are fragile; equally, some museums have small collections specifically for students to touch and explore.

Be aware that some heritage sites can be hazardous: steep staircases, low entrances, uneven floors, crumbling masonry. And do check whether sites are wheelchair accessible or suitable for disabled students.

# Starter questions for heritage sites

It's important to get students 'in the mood'. What aspects of heritage sites do they find most unfamiliar or fascinating? Toilet facilities (or lack of them), dungeons and gory details usually come top!

Asking a few warm up questions will help get students thinking about the people who lived at the site. Perhaps they'll find that their ancestors are closer to them in behaviour and interests than they expected.

- When do you think this was built? By whom? Why? How?
- What do you think it was used for? What do you think it looked like originally?
- What do you think it was like to live here? Why are doorways so low? How did people live without bathrooms and toilets/fridges/TVs or radios/microwaves/cars/shops/plastic or metal/modern medicine/chocolate/cigarettes/football?
- What would it have looked/smelled/sounded like when these people lived here?
- Would you like to live here? Why/why not?

# Model-mapping

You could try making a 'map' of the heritage site that you visit. It will help students explain and extend their thinking. You could start by simply asking 'Who lived here?' and 'Why?'. Many different ideas can spring from this activity.

Alongside is an example of how a map with different questions might look for this activity.

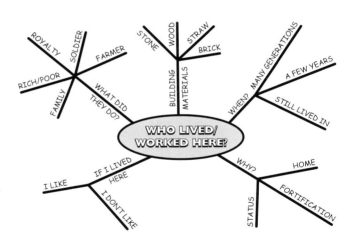

# Example map of Stonehenge

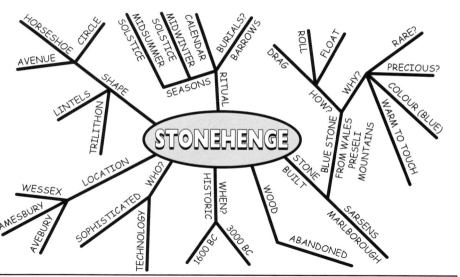

# Cross-curricular opportunities

School trips are valuable experiences for students in their own right, but they also provide opportunities for exciting cross-curricular work.

For example, a visit to an art gallery can feed into many subjects:

**Science** – Sir Joseph Wright's *An experiment on a bird with the air pump*, 1768. What does this painting tell us about the development of science at this particular time?

**Geography** – JMW Turner's *Sunrise through vapour*, 1804. How accurate is this representation of the Lake District? Can you tell if the valley is glaciated or formed by river erosion? How has the landscape changed since 1804?

**Citizenship** – Stanley Spencer's Sandham Memorial Chapel, 1920s, Burghclere. What was Spencer's attitude to war? What did he want to communicate to his audience? Do you think he succeeded?

# Field trips

When it comes to field trips you will have all the planning required for 'indoor' trips, with additional concerns such as the vagaries of British weather, equipment and hazards associated with the outdoors.

Even in summer, as a minimum, students should have:

- Comfortable walking boots
- Waterproof clothing
- A rucksack or other hands-free bag
- Water and food
- Map of area (group leaders should carry a compass)
- Plastic bags (for sitting on damp ground and carrying samples), notebook and pencils
- Sunscreen and headgear

At least one person in a group should have a mobile phone and a first aid kit – usually the adult supervisor.

# Collecting samples

If you intend to collect samples (leaves, insects, soil, fossils) you will need to get permission from the landowner. Many sites, for example National Trust properties, request that children do not take anything back to school and leave everything as they found it. Remind children not to disturb animal burrows or nests.

This doesn't mean that you can't handle samples or record them with sketches or photographs. Just be aware that your activities may be restricted. Always check before you visit.

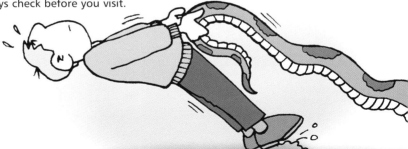

# Successful worksheets

Before the trip, discuss with students what you expect them to achieve by the end of the visit. Good worksheets give a framework for the day and help students to focus on key objectives.

Avoid cramming in too many activities where children are rushing from one question to the next. Allow them time to reflect on what they have seen and to enjoy the experience.

- Develop activities that are open-ended
- Don't try to do too much – concentrate on three or four areas/artefacts in depth
- Structure worksheets to support future work/research

Encourage students to consider the context of the site/artefact and think about its contribution to the world – what does it tell us about how people live(d) and what is/was important to them? What does it tell us about how the presence of people has altered the landscape?

# Extension activities

Follow-up work helps children gain a more in-depth understanding of the object/work of art/heritage site that they have seen. Here are some suggestions for cross-curricular work.

- If you were going to be painted by this artist, what would you want in the background/to have around you to demonstrate your interests and personality? What props might you use if you were to be painted in a studio rather than 'on location'?
- Paintings/sketches/collages/photographs/videos/diaries/letters/newspaper reports/ narrative/poetry/drama/non-fiction/fiction/explanation 'in the style of ...'/'at the time of ...', and so on
- Dramatic reconstruction of the 'story' in the painting/object or event at the heritage site
- You could have a go at some practical investigation. For example, how did a Roman catapult work? How did Stone Age people make flour/bread?

# Business and commerce

You can use the same approaches for visiting a commercial business or factory as you would for a cultural site but there are some differences.

Be clear about the purpose of the visit – there may be more than one:

- To prepare students for work experience/the world of work
- To experience how classroom work can be applied in the real world
- To help students learn about businesses in their area and how they contribute to the community
- To advise the company on youth issues
- To help with market research

# Being business-like

When planning a trip to a local business, discuss appropriate behaviour with your students, reminding them that employees will still be working during their visit.

The type of business will affect the way students dress (especially if they are not in uniform). The staff of some companies adopt more formal dress than others. Students should conform to the company's norm as far as possible, as a mark of respect.

Check to see if any safety equipment, such as hard hats, is required. If so, can the company provide it?

# Pre-planning for visits to businesses

Pre-planning is crucial so students know exactly what to expect and what to do when they arrive at the chosen company. Unless you are visiting a factory or other manufacturing site, there may be very little to see beyond a lot of people sitting at computers. It's unlikely that a banking company will let your party into the vaults to look at the cash – but you never know!

Discuss the aims and objectives of the visit with students:

- Fact-finding/research
- An on-going Education Business Partnership [www.nebpn.org]
- Help with a particular aspect of business enterprise: sales and marketing, budgeting, production, fundraising [www.young-enterprise.org.uk]

Research the company you are going to visit: look at their website and annual report. Encourage students to prepare questions then plan your worksheet accordingly. Remind students of health and safety rules, eg not touching machinery or equipment.

# Asking difficult questions

Let the company's education officer know what specific area of their business you want to look at. This is particularly important if students want to discuss **environmental issues or business ethics**.

Students should be given the opportunity to ask difficult questions, but it's usually best to send them in advance of the visit to give the company ample opportunity to research their answers. The person who accompanies your students on their visit may not know off-hand how many tonnes of hardwood are cut down in Amazonian rain forests, but given the chance they may find out.

This also gives students the opportunity to discuss difficult business decisions. Why not ask the company to give students some real-life situations to role-play, either in advance of the visit or as extension activities? Then find out what the company actually did.

# Developing the business relationship

It's important for students to feel involved with the company. If possible, discuss with the education officer how students can contribute.

- Is there some technical problem that students can try to solve?
- Can students help with marketing or market research?
- What opportunities are there for work experience?
- Can students work with company staff to plan fundraising for school, for example?

Most businesses want to be involved with local communities. Be creative in developing relationships. It doesn't have to be one way!

# Outdoor and Activity Trips

# Outdoor and activity trips

### Outdoor activities

For some children this will be the most exciting activity they've ever done; for others it will be a source of concern. You could ask an older pupil who's already been on the trip to give a talk about what to expect.

### Adventure activities

Even if you are not leading the activity, as the trip organiser you and other teachers are ultimately responsible for students – even where instruction is by an external course provider. Make sure that:

- Leaders and supervisors of adventure activities hold the relevant National Governing Body (NGB) award where it exists and get this in writing

- The provider is familiar with the Adventure Activities Licensing Regulations 1996. The AALA regulates many of the most potentially hazardous activities, but if your school provides activities for its own pupils it has no inspection/licensing powers

- You check to see if your LEA has separate procedures for approving the competence or experience of an activity leader

# Disabled pupils

In many cases, there's no reason why physically disabled pupils shouldn't be included on outdoor activity trips. Make sure you include any special needs in your risk assessment and seek advice from your LEA's or activity centre's disability officer.

www.calvert-trust.org.uk organise outdoor activities for disabled people as well as disability awareness courses.

# Risk assessment for adventure activities

Many of the key aspects of risk assessment are explained on pages 86-92 but there are some differences when it comes to water-based and adventure activities.

- Your school retains the overall 'duty of care' for students but you don't have to do a detailed risk assessment for the activities involved when you are using staff from an AALA centre

- Your job is to **check that the activity provider has carried out the necessary risk assessments** and has relevant safety management plans in place with appropriately qualified people. It's a good idea to ask your LEA's OEA to advise you on this

- Always take local advice and have a contingency if you need to change your plans. For example, if the river you were going to canoe down is dangerously swollen, go hiking/cycling instead. Make sure you have a risk assessment for this new activity

# Coastal visits

A trip to the seaside! Lovely! But even students who are brought up near the coast need to be reminded of potential hazards. Your risk assessment should consider: tide-times, rips, sewage outfalls, areas of soft sand, cliffs, land slips, falling rocks and rogue waves. (The same rules apply for other areas of natural water.) It's also helpful to explain the conditions of the beach: rocky, sandy, stony, or muddy.

- Make a note of any poor or non-swimmers within the group
- You should have at least one supervisor for every 10 students (or more for younger students – see page 106)
- Ensure students understand any flag system in operation; be aware of any restricted areas and how and where to call for help
- Students should only enter the water in recognised bathing areas with lifeguard cover and stay within sight and shouting distance of lifeguard and supervisors
- At least one supervisor should be the 'lookout' on dry land and at least one adult member of staff should have a life saving award

# Farm visits

Farms are marvellous places for students to learn about the countryside and food production. Standing 'in your breakfast' in the middle of a cereal crop is an amazing concept to some. Choose a farm that is used to school parties and has a good reputation for health and safety and animal welfare. You will also need:

- Hand-washing facilities and suitable toilet areas
- Somewhere safe to eat and drink

Students need clear guidelines about what they can/can't do and can/can't touch. Here are some simple rules:

- Don't put your fingers or face near an animal's mouth
- Don't rub your face against animals' fur
- Don't put your hands in your mouth after feeding an animal
- Always wash your hands before eating
- Don't eat any animal food (!) or drink from outdoor taps
- Don't touch or go near farm machinery

# Leading a skiing trip

If you're a keen skier or snowboarder then you may well be considering taking a school group on a skiing trip. For many students, the school trip is their first experience of skiing and can lead to a lifelong passion.

But being an enthusiast is just the start. To lead a school ski trip you need a recognised qualification – no matter how experienced a skier you are. Your LEA may run courses, or you can contact one of the companies providing the four main courses on offer:

- Ski Course Organiser: two days with the English Ski Council's Schools and Youth Committee or a more advanced six-day course for the experienced skier
- Alpine Ski Leader: a seven-day course with Snowsport Scotland
- Snowboard Leader: a six-day course with Snowsport Scotland concentrating on snowboarding

There is no law regarding the wearing of helmets but it is good practice for pupils to do so. Sweden and Norway offer free lift passes to children wearing helmets.

# Instructing on skiing trips

If you wish to coach students on skiing trips, you will need a British Association of Ski Instructors (BASI) qualification.

Outside the UK, not all ski schools are regulated. Check that your students' instructor has a qualification validated by the International Ski Instructors' Association.

For additional information, have a look at some of these dedicated skiing websites:

- www.bssoa.co.uk
- www.fis-ski.com
- www.skihealth.com

(See chapter 5 for information on overseas trips.)

# Unsupervised or remote groups

You may have a group of students who need to be left unsupervised as part of their chosen activity, eg Duke of Edinburgh's Award, or orienteering. If you are planning this, you must seek parental consent before the trip.

Prepare students gradually, introducing the skills necessary for self-reliance and responsibility. You could do this in several stages:

- Do a trial run with students, then shadow them while they are working
- Progress to meeting them regularly at agreed locations
- Then meet occasionally, allowing them unsupervised time

Check that students have the correct equipment and clothing and that they are fully aware of health and safety regulations, how to get help, and what to do in an emergency. It is advisable that at least one person in the group has a mobile phone. However, don't rely on this as in some remote areas it is not possible to get a signal.

# Residential visits – communicating with parents

It's important to involve parents in educational trips, particularly when you are planning to take their child away from home overnight, maybe for the first time.

Invite them to a meeting where details of the proposed visit are explained. Provide written information too, not forgetting parents who are unable to attend the meeting. (You may need to have written material translated for EAL parents.)

List likely issues or concerns before meeting parents and be as open as possible. Encourage questions and deal sympathetically and professionally with any concerns.

# Residential visits – FAQs

Typically, the kinds of questions parents ask include the following:

- Will my child be able to phone/email home during the visit?
- What happens if they don't like it and want to come home?
- My child has never shared a room before. What if they find it difficult to cope?
- How will you deal with homesickness?
- I do not wish my daughter to mix with boys. How will you enforce this?
- Will there be groups from other schools/establishments? Who? What age?
- How will you arrange for my child to go to church/temple/mosque while away?
- My child is vegetarian/only eats halal food/hates spinach? Will this be a problem?
- I don't want Saffy sharing a room with xyz. How will you sort out room-sharing?

# Residential visits – information for group leaders

It's a big responsibility being the group leader for a residential visit. Your support team should include **at least one teacher for every 10 students** and at least one male and one female teacher for mixed groups. Consider also:

- Adult accommodation should be next to the students'
- Do you need a torch? For example on campsites
- Male and female sleeping/bathroom facilities (students' and adults') should be separate and exclusively for the group's use
- Security arrangements should stop unauthorised visitors – students' rooms should not be on the ground floor
- Have the hostel staff been checked as suitable for work with young people?
- Do you have appropriate access to students' rooms? (Doors should be lockable)
- Has the hostel got washing and drying facilities, plus storage for clothes, luggage, equipment and valuables?
- Check fire exits/instructions – hold a fire drill shortly after arrival
- What provision is there for students with special needs or those who become ill?

# Competencies for group leaders

There are two types of competence required for group leaders: technical and pastoral. Both can be incorporated into your role as group leader or you can split the responsibilities with another member of staff. **Even if you take on both roles yourself, you will still need a competent, trained assistant.**

**Technical responsibilities**
- Plan, manage and lead activities – conduct the risk assessment
- Have appropriate level of experience and qualifications

**Pastoral**
- Manage the care, welfare and experience of students according to age, ability and needs
- Have a recognised qualification, such as teacher or youth worker

Technical decisions can be informed by, but should not be overruled by, pastoral issues.

# Notes

**Getting Started**

 **General Tips for Successful Trips**

 **Trips for Culture and Commerce**

 **Outdoor and Activity Trips**

 **Overseas and Exchange Trips** ◄

 **Health and Safety**

 **School Trips and the Law**

 **Further Information**

# Overseas and Exchange Trips

# We're all going on a summer holiday!

We all want to switch into holiday mode the minute we step out of school, but there's a lot of preparation you can do to make the trip more enjoyable for you and your students.

Much of the advice for trips in the UK applies to overseas trips. But there are some additional considerations. Again, a minimum of one adult to 10 students is sensible but at least two of the adults should be teachers with an appropriate male/female mix. Make sure you have enough adults to cover an emergency.

Spend some time studying the culture and customs of the country you are to visit. Discuss expectations of behaviour or dress, particularly at religious sites (and it's easier to quickly identify students if they all wear uniform/matching baseball hats/backpacks). You may also need to discuss attitudes to females in some countries.

One of the adults in your group should have a working knowledge of the language – if not, consider hiring a local translator.

# Pupil behaviour

Take time to discuss the **reasons** for a code of behaviour as well as ensuring that students understand it. Typically, students will be expected to:

- Follow your instructions or those of the person supervising them
- Avoid unnecessary risks and report them to you or their supervisor
- Dress appropriately for conditions (and be sensitive to any local customs)

Equally, they will be expected not to:

- Bring or try to gain access to non-prescription drugs, alcohol or offensive materials
- Bring items of value
- Engage in sexual activity (either with fellow students or local people)
- Behave inappropriately both in private and in public (this includes kissing/cuddling)

And if you're going to ask students to abide by these rules, they also have to apply to staff and adult volunteers!

# Tour operators and organising your own transport

Make sure **your operator** is a member of ABTA (Association of British Travel Agents). This will give you some protection if things go wrong. Also, be sure you have comprehensive travel insurance.

If you use a tour operator, you are a customer and protected by H&S laws, trade description legislation, and package holiday regulations.  Most major companies in the school travel business belong to STF, the School Travel Forum (www.lastuk.org). Do remember, though, that the Adventure Activities Licensing Authority (AALA) does not inspect or license overseas providers.

If you are organising **your own transport**, check that drivers are familiar with the vehicle, the rules of the country you are visiting, and right-hand driving. As group leader, be aware that a left-hand drive vehicle will have the door on the 'wrong' side for disembarkation – a potential hazard.

Contact the Department of Transport (www.dtlr.gov.uk) for further information.

# Choosing a tour operator

Many companies now offer educational visits, so how do you choose what's right for your pupils?  First, **ensure it is reputable**.  Is the tour package covered by ATOL? The DTI approves 7 'bonding' bodies:

- Association of British Travel Agents (ABTA)
- Federation of Tour Operators Trust (FTOT)
- Passenger Shipping Association (PSA)
- The Confederation of Passenger Transport (CPT)
- Yacht Charter Association (YCA)
- The Association of Bonded Travel Organisers Trust (ABTOT)

Other helpful resources:

- The Schools and Group Travel Association (01989 567690)
- The School Journey Association (020 8765 6636)
- The Suzy Lamplugh Trust's book *World Wise* (www.suzylamplugh.org)

# Vaccinations and first aid

If the country you visit is particularly hazardous in terms of infection and disease you will need to take more extensive precautions than a basic first aid kit. Check the Department of Health website (www.dh.gov.uk) for up-to-date information.

- Are any vaccinations required? If so, inform students and parents in good time
- Does the country you will be visiting require proof of vaccination? Check the DoH (see above) and Foreign and Commonwealth Office websites (www.fco.gov.uk) before travelling

You will also need to pack a more comprehensive first aid kit. Again, the DoH can advise you on any recommended medication, needles and syringes.

Remember, airlines have very strict rules about taking sharp instruments on to aeroplanes, so do check that you have appropriate paperwork for your first aid kit. This may be in the form of a letter from the school/doctor. Check with your travel operator/airline.

# Documentation

**Visas/Passports**

At an early stage, check that students have valid passports and visas or use a group passport. Do you have any students who are not British? During your planning process check what regulations apply to them.

In case these documents are stolen or mislaid while you are away, take photocopies or scan passports and email them to an accessible account. This is a useful tip for all vital documentation. Most countries have internet cafes in urban areas.

**Form E111**

This form is available from post offices and entitles the holder to free or cheaper medical treatment in the EU. It must be completed by the child's parent/carer – and don't forget to make copies to be left at school.

# Planning for culture shock

An exchange visit is an excellent way for a pupil to learn about the language and culture of another country. But things don't always go smoothly; the lifestyle of host families can be so different from a pupil's own experiences.

- Invite students and parents to a meeting to discuss any queries they may have about having a guest from another country in their home and vice versa
- Perhaps a teacher from the host school could attend or a pupil who has been on a previous exchange could give a short presentation

**Hola**

Encourage students to discuss the forthcoming exchange.

**Pleased to meet you**

- There may be language difficulties but even where there aren't, the culture, behaviour and 'house rules' can be hard for students to understand
- Discussing these 'rules' can be the basis for students to prepare a scrapbook or video diary about their own family to send to the host family overseas. It will help the host family to know what to expect

**Buon giorno**

**Bonjour**

**Wilkommen**  **Hey Dude!**

# My house rules

Before the visit, encourage students to discuss some of the 'rules' in their own households to help them get a better understanding of the ways in which families can differ, eg in my house:

- We have to use the back door and leave our shoes outside
- I have to walk the dog before tea
- We call the evening meal 'tea' not 'dinner' and I take turns with my brother to lay the table and do the washing up
- We all eat at different times – usually in front of the TV
- I have to do my homework before I can watch TV/use the computer
- Bed time is 10.30pm and 11pm at weekends
- We are all vegetarian/only eat halal/kosher food

# Strange food

One of the biggest potential areas of conflict is food. Whilst UK eating habits are diverse and heavily influenced by different cultures, many children have food 'fads'. And it's not just young children either. Health- or size-conscious teenagers may revolt at the idea of three meals a day instead of salad and black coffee or water.

When students email their host families, get them to collect local recipes. It may not be possible for the school canteen to try them out, but some can be made at students' homes and brought into school for 'tasting parties'.

Whilst you don't want to encourage students to be faddy eaters, it's probably better that host families know in advance if there are any foods that students won't eat – wasting a full plate of food can cause offence.

# Minimising potential conflict

Developing good relations with the partner school will help – use email and scrapbooks/video diaries to help students communicate with each other before beginning the exchange.

You can also minimise conflicts by:

- Agreeing ground rules between you as group leader, the students and the host family, including telephone/email contact with you and their parents/carers. (A BT contact card allows calls home to be charged to the parents' number from anywhere in the world)
- Matching students to children of similar age, gender, interests
- Taking into account any medical/dietary/special needs of students and checking host families can cope with this
- Making clear arrangements for collecting and returning students to families, and for any events arranged during the visit

# Exchange family breakdown

It can happen that exchange families and their guest cannot get on. Whatever the reason for this you should have a contingency plan: is there another family who could take this pupil?

You should also plan how you would manage if a pupil needed to be sent home:

- Are tickets transferable or will a charge be made? Who will pay for this?
- Do you have enough staff to allow for someone to escort the pupil home?
- Will their parents/carers be there to meet them or have they gone on holiday?

This situation is rare, but it does happen occasionally. So plan in advance: expect the worst and hope for the best!

Keep a list of all host families' names and addresses and remember: host families are not subject to English law.

# The return visit

Get as much feedback as possible from the host school and encourage students to stay in touch by email. Agree a plan for the exchange visit, taking into account:

- Do the exchange staff have any particular sites they would like to see? For example, London, Alton Towers or Stonehenge
- Do exchange students have any special requirements?
- Are there more children returning a visit than you sent out? Do you have spare/ emergency host families? Can some families take more than one guest?

It is useful for the visiting school to know in advance about your school, eg ethos, curriculum, timetable. Perhaps some of your colleagues would be interested in producing a video or scrapbook about your town: location, history, places of interest.

The return visit should be more straightforward as the families and students have already met, but do check relationships are still acceptable and whether circumstances have changed. A new baby in the family, bereavement, or a parent losing their job can all affect whether having an exchange guest is still practical.

# Trips to remote areas or developing countries

For older students this can be a chance to be really challenged and to experience very different cultural norms from those with which they are familiar. Trekking in Nepal or walking through the Amazon can be life-changing events. But both students and parents need to understand what 'challenging' means in this context and what level of fitness is required.

Invite students and parents to a meeting to discuss the proposed trip and explain your approach to risk assessment and how you plan to minimise potential hazards. Hazards could be emotional, cultural or psychological rather than simply physical, eg seeing terrible poverty or death first hand, or visiting the site of a battlefield.

If the proposed visit site is particularly remote, how could local rescue services respond to an emergency, life-threatening illness or group evacuation?

Check the Code of Practice for Youth Expeditions produced by the Young Explorers Trust (www.theyet.org).

Getting Started

 General Tips for Successful Trips

 Trips for Culture and Commerce

 Outdoor and Activity Trips

 Overseas and Exchange Trips

 Health and Safety

 School Trips and the Law

 Further Information

# Health and Safety

# Risk assessment

For any trip away from school grounds you will need to do a risk assessment.
Even regular trips, eg swimming, should have frequently updated risk assessments.*
Ask yourself these questions:

1. Have I considered any possible hazards?
2. Who might be harmed by these hazards – and how?
3. Have I evaluated the risks?
4. Have I recorded my findings and given them to my EVC/headteacher/ governors/LEA?
5. Have I reviewed my risk assessment? Do I need to revise it?

Always list:

- Appropriate group size
- Age and ability
- Staff supervision and leadership responsibility
- Emergency procedures

*There are additional considerations for water-based or adventure activities (page 60).*

# 1. Possible hazards on school trips

> *\* chemicals \* dangerous tools \* machinery \* building work \* traffic \**
> *water hazards \*weather conditions \* difficulty of activity \* farm animals \**
> *cliffs \* transport \* pickpockets \**

Hazards can come in so many different forms and may be dependent on the age of your students. You will need to consider:

- Size/make up of the group
- Site you plan to visit/accommodation/food. Is the site remote from emergency services? (For field trips, it is good practice to inform the local emergency services giving OS map references where possible.)
- What are the planned activities during the trip and who is running them? Are they experienced/appropriately qualified?
- What transport arrangements have been made? Are they adequate/safe?
- What if you are unable to speak the language on overseas trips? How would you/students/staff communicate in an emergency?

# 2. Who might be harmed?

All age groups are prone to wandering off – even your adult supervisors! But ask yourself who is particularly vulnerable?

- Do any of the students/staff have disabilities, special needs or medical problems?
- How would the group be affected if a pupil needed to withdraw or go home?

# 3. Evaluating the risk

It's almost impossible to eliminate risk, but you can minimise it. If you can't visit the site beforehand, get as much information as you can from a range of sources and have at least one first aider for every group of students. Each LEA sets its own ratio according to type of trip. Ask yourself these key questions:

- What must I do to reduce risk to an acceptable level and how can I monitor risk during the trip?
- What emergency measures should I put in place?

# 4. Put your risk assessment in writing

When you have completed your risk assessment give copies to your headteacher/EVC/governors/LEA (as required by your school policy) and all visit supervisors. You must be able to demonstrate that:

- You have made a proper check – including a check of any third parties who will be involved with students
- You have considered possible hazards, who might be affected by them and how to minimise their impact
- The precautions you intend to take are reasonable and any remaining risk is low

# 5. Reviewing your assessment

This may become necessary because a new piece of information has become available to you. For example, you have been able to make a site visit or you have learned that one pupil has a particular difficulty with an aspect of the trip.

It is important that you review your risk assessment at this point.

Remember, risk assessments are not just to provide an audit trail, they are the means by which you intend to keep students and staff safe during the visit.

All the same, don't become too obsessed with detail. The HSE recommends that risk assessments should be **uncomplicated** and easy for everyone to understand. The law requires your risk assessment to be **suitable and sufficient** – not perfect.

# School trips and the law

## The Paul Ellis Case

Paul Ellis pleaded guilty to manslaughter after a pupil drowned on a school trip in 2003. During sentencing the judge told him he had been, 'unbelievably foolhardy and negligent'.

- The river was swollen by heavy rain
- The water was -8°C
- There was no rope: pupils knotted towels together during the rescue attempt
- A teacher from another school had warned Paul Ellis that the pool was dangerous
- An RAF training team had earlier decided the pool was too dangerous for swimming.

Basic safety procedure was ignored. A simple risk assessment could have prevented this tragedy.

# Risk assessment action plan

This simple table will help you with your planning.

| Activity/hazard/situation | Action required | By whom | By when |
|---|---|---|---|
| | | | |
| | | | |
| | | | |
| | | | |
| | | | |
| | | | |
| | | | |

Signed .......................................................................... Date ...........................

# Administering medication

You may have students who need medication or who have severe allergic reactions to certain foods or to bee stings. Always take advice from students' GPs.

On a medical consent form parents/carers must give you information on any medical condition and request that medication be administered. Ask for name of medication, dose, method of administration, time and frequency, possible side effects. Don't give aspirin to children under 16 unless advised by a doctor.

Although you are not contractually required to give medication or to supervise a pupil taking it, you must have someone who has received **appropriate training from a medically qualified person** to fulfil this role on trips. Ideally, two adults should be present when medication is administered.

The school's **insurance** (if appropriate) should fully indemnify **staff and volunteers** against claims for alleged negligence, but avoid taking students to hospital in your own car – you may not have the necessary car insurance and could be guilty of negligence.

*Supporting Students with Medical Needs* is available from the DfES.

# First aid

If you are the trip leader, you shouldn't be responsible for first aid as well. Make sure you have another adult with you to take on this role.

The main duties of a first aider are to:

- Check that the first aid kit is appropriately stocked
- Help people with common injuries or illnesses immediately
- If necessary, call for an ambulance or other professional medical help

Your risk assessor and first aider should also consider these questions:

- What injuries might occur from this activity? How could they be treated with first aid?
- Where is the nearest hospital?

# Training for the first aider

A four-day First Aid at Work certificate is appropriate for teachers working outdoors. But remember, first aid certificates are only valid for **three years**. Refresher training should take place at least three months before the certificate expiry date.

**Basic training**
- Contents of a first aid box
- Managing an incident/emergency
- Control of bleeding
- Resuscitation – as appropriate for age group
- Health and safety for employers and employees
- Treatment of unconscious casualties

It is also useful for the first aider on field trips to have taken the Rescue Emergency Care (REC) course and/or the two-day Far From Help or Expedition First Aid training.

# General first aid for staff on trips

It's a good idea for all staff and, where possible, all adults who go on trips to know what to do in an emergency:

- CPR (cardiopulmonary resuscitation)
- First aid for people who are unconscious, wounded or bleeding

**Contents of a first aid kit**
You can buy pre-packed first aid kits from pharmacies. By law, minibuses must carry a first aid kit. There is a minimum requirement for trips:

- 20 individually-wrapped sterile adhesive dressings (mixed sizes)
- A leaflet giving general advice on first aid
- One large sterile unmedicated wound dressing
- Two triangular bandages
- Two safety pins
- Individually-wrapped moist cleansing wipes
- One pair of disposable gloves

Additional items may be necessary for specialised activities.

# Reporting accidents

If anything happens to a pupil or colleague, follow your LEA/school guidelines
and make sure you keep a record of any first aid given, including:

- Date, time and place
- Name and class of the injured/ill person
- Details of the injury/illness
- What happened to the person immediately afterwards (went home, carried on, went to hospital)
- Name and signature of the first aider or appointed person

**Fatal or major injuries and dangerous occurrences must be reported immediately**
(by telephone) to the HSE. You will also need to complete Form 2508.
(Details from www.hse.gov.uk/pubns/edis1.htm)

# Minibuses and coaches

Coaches and minibuses that carry three or more children between 3 and 15 years of age must be fitted with a seat belt for each child and comply with legal requirements. Ensure students use the seatbelts. The seats must face forward. And remember, all minibuses are required by law to carry a first aid kit.

# Mobile phones

By law, you can't use a hand-held mobile phone whilst driving. You are allowed to use a hands-free set, but RoSPA suggests that employers adopt this advice:

'You must not make or receive a call on a mobile phone (whether hand-held or hands-free) as the driver of a vehicle unless it is parked in a safe place. No line-manager shall require an employee to receive a call on a mobile phone whilst driving. Contravention of these requirements will be regarded as a serious disciplinary matter.'

# Driving minibuses

For many trips, the school minibus will be all you need. This is particularly true for PE fixtures and A-Level field trips. But it will certainly take the pressure off you if you can hire a coach/minibus and driver. If this isn't possible, then you need to take note of the rules and regulations:

- School minibuses are operated under a permit and cannot be driven by teachers under the age of 21. However, some LEAs have raised this to 23 or even 25 years and you will need to take their test (about £50) and re-take it every three years
- If you passed your (car) test after 1997 then you will need to take a DVLA course and a test – costing around £600. It may be worthwhile to ask to take this course as part of your continuing professional development. If you passed your test before 1.1.97 you are not required by law to undergo further training or tests although most LEAs recommend further training

A free booklet on minibus driving is available from the Institute of Advanced Motorists Tel: 0845 310 8311.

# Keeping track of students

Before setting off on your trip, your supervisors should have a list of the students for whom they are responsible. For younger students it's advisable to make sure their clothing is distinctive and highly visible, for example brightly-coloured baseball caps or backpacks, preferably carrying the name of the school.

1 2 3 4...

School uniform also makes students easy to spot but may not be practical for field trips. However, if you ask students to wear badges with the name of the school, don't let them put their first name or family name on the badges. This makes it all too easy for a 'friendly' stranger to begin a conversation with them.

It may sound obvious, but you should always carry out a head count before leaving any venue.

Getting Started

 General Tips for Successful Trips

 Trips for Culture and Commerce

 Outdoor and Activity Trips

 Overseas and Exchange Trips

 Health and Safety

 School Trips and the Law

 Further Information

# School Trips and the Law

# Understanding the law

Some schools are seriously considering whether they should continue with school trips in light of the case where a teacher was sentenced to 12 months in prison for manslaughter when a pupil in his care died on a school trip (see page 91).

It would be a great shame if schools stopped taking students on trips, but planning, close monitoring and an understanding of the law will help you to make informed decisions.

Both civil law and criminal law govern the rules for educational visits:

- **Civil law** entitles victims to seek compensation from the person or employer of the person who caused them injury/loss
- Under **criminal law**, penalties are given to the person who has broken the law. This could be a fine or imprisonment

# Negligence

Whoever plans your school policy for trips and for response to emergency situations should have compared these management systems with other schools and with LEA regulations. There is a very good reason for this.

Should an accident/incident occur that leads to litigation, if your policy/response can be shown to be inferior to that of another school in a similar situation, this could lead to a challenge of negligence.

Culpability is defined by the nature of the activity and the level of risk involved. Inexperience cannot be used as a defence.

# What does the law mean for school trips?

Failing to meet health and safety requirements **without good cause** is negligence. This is why it's so important to carry out a risk assessment for your proposed trip.

### Duty of care
The phrase *in loco parentis* isn't correct – you are not there in place of a parent. As a teacher you have neither the responsibilities nor powers of a parent, but schools do owe students a 'duty of care'. This is a legal duty to consider and look after the welfare and safety of students.

### Standard of care
This is defined as doing 'what is reasonable in all the circumstances of the case for the purpose of safeguarding or promoting the child's welfare' and as a teacher you must use **reasonable care and skill**.

# Staff code of conduct

On any trip you will discuss with students what is appropriate and inappropriate behaviour. Students and their parents should fully understand the rules and agree to them in writing.

Of course, staff are also bound by a professional code but you will need to devise a code of behaviour for any adult supervisors. This can be a sensitive issue for your volunteer helpers, but by explaining that everyone on the trip has a code of behaviour, you should be able to deal with any problems.

As a minimum the adult behaviour code should state that staff/supervisors must not:

- Allow students to stay at their home unsupervised *even in an emergency*
- Allow or join in sexually provocative games – even horseplay
- Make sexual comments about a pupil either in public or private
- Make assumptions about students or jump to conclusions – always check facts

# Adult:pupil ratios

For each trip you should assess any possible risks and decide on a safe and appropriate adult:pupil ratio – but you need to be aware that there are minimum requirements.

- **Years 1 - 3**         one adult for every six students and a higher ratio for reception classes
- **Years 4 - 6**         one adult for every 10-15 students
- **Year 7 upwards**    one adult for every 15-20 students

However, a higher ratio is a good idea in crowded or busy urban areas, or in potentially high-risk locations.

# Insurance

Insurance is a difficult issue because there are so many different types including:

- Employers' liability
- Public liability
- Personal accident cover for students, teachers, parents or other adults
- Compensation for loss of baggage and personal effects including money up to a fixed amount
- Costs of medical treatment or flight home in the case of serious illness or injury
- High-risk activities such as skiing – usually excluded from basic policies
- Damage to or loss of hired equipment (check the small print)
- Unplanned or emergency transport/accommodation
- Compensation against cancellation or delay
- Bankruptcy of travel agent/operator
- Legal help/costs

# Insurance for your school trip

Your EVC can organise insurance cover, but **a school is not under a duty to arrange insurance for its staff and students**.  However, as group leader you must ensure that adequate insurance arrangements are in place.

- Clarify with your LEA what insurance provision already exists and any additional insurance required, eg public liability insurance
- Tell parents the scope of any insurance arranged by the school, underlining what you are/are not responsible for

If you are not going to organise insurance through the school, make sure you give parents plenty of warning that they will need to get insurance. Put this in your parents' consent form (see page 113).

A specialist school travel operator will help you find the right kind of insurance. This is important where activities may be harzardous, eg skiing or water sports.

# Complaints procedure

When you are communicating with parents/students you will need to inform them of your school's complaints procedure. You may consider giving this out with the trip information sheet (page 113).

Your school policy should take into account:

- When does a gripe become a complaint? How will you record it?
- Who receives complaints? What are their responsibilities/chain of information? How will information be managed?
- What procedures are in place to protect and support the pupil/member of staff involved?
- What timescale is appropriate for dealing with complaints?
- If the complaint is upheld, what steps can the school take to avoid it happening again?

# Approval for educational visits

Once you have planned your visit you need to supplement informal permission with written approval from your headteacher, governors or LEA. Your LEA may have a special form for this. Next you must obtain parental consent. Copies of the key information should be passed to your EVC but **always take copies with you** on your trip.

- Purpose of visit/educational objectives
- Location of trip, accommodation, date/times
- Size, age and m/f composition of the group; any medical or special needs
- Educational objectives/programme of activities, including risk assessment
- Names of staff and volunteer supervisors (include any information on useful qualifications/experience); contact details of person at school holding information in case of emergency
- Transport arrangements/travel operator (including licence/reference numbers)
- Budget
- Insurance arrangements and policy number/details
- Parental consent forms

Signed _____ Date _____ Headteacher_____ Date _____

Getting Started

 General Tips for
Successful Trips

 Trips for Culture
and Commerce

 Outdoor and
Activity Trips

 Overseas and
Exchange Trips

 Health and
Safety

 School Trips
and the Law

 Further
Information

# Further
# Information

# Parental consent

When you're communicating with parents about school trips (and make sure you get consent from both parents if they are divorced/separated), it's important to give as much information as possible so they can make informed decisions about their child's participation. It also shows that you have thought through any possible complications.

A parental consent form should be completed for each pupil in the group, including children who have carers or who are in care. You do need to seek specific consent for:

- Any non-routine visit for students in Years 1 - 3
- Adventure activities
- Residential visits/visits abroad
- Remote supervision

Unless your school has specifically taken care of this, you will also need to warn parents in advance of a trip of any insurance requirements that they will need to arrange. (See page 108).

# Parents' consent form

It's important that you get as much information as possible about students as well as parents' **medical consent**. UK doctors will still carry out emergency treatment without parental consent, but it is sensible to have it available and it may be a necessity when abroad. If parents do not agree to this, you may have to consider withdrawing the child from the trip.

When you give out the parents' consent form, include an information sheet about the trip and an email/phone number for parents to contact you with any individual queries.

Details of visit to......................
Depart: date/time.......................
Return: date/time.......................

I agree to.........................................taking part in this visit
and to the activities described. I have read the
information sheet and understand that.................must
behave responsibly. If for any reason my child is sent
home, I will be informed......................beforehand.

☐ I have organised insurance for my child for this
trip. [IF RELEVANT]

Information about my child
Birth date.................. NHS number.....................
GP's Name/address/phone.................................
...............................................................

Please list any conditions requiring medication.
...............................................................

How far can your child swim without flotation aids?
50m 200m 500m other...........................................

# Residential visits/exchanges

Has your son/daughter been in contact with anything, or suffered from any condition in the last four weeks that may be contagious or infectious? Yes/No.
If YES please give brief details
.................................................................................................................

.................................................................................................................

Is your son/daughter allergic to any medication? Yes/No. If YES, please specify
.................................................................................................................

When did your son/daughter last have a tetanus injection?
.................................................................................................................

Does your son/daughter have any phobias? Yes/No. If YES, please specify
.................................................................................................................

Does your son/daughter have any additional special needs, eg: dietary requirements, travel sickness, toileting problems, sleep walking, night terrors, other?
Please specify.......................................................................................................
I will promptly inform...............................of any changes between now and the visit.

# Always include these statements

There are some legal phrases that you should include in all parental consent forms for school trips:

- I agree to my son/daughter receiving medication as instructed and any emergency dental, medical or surgical treatment (including blood transfusion/anaesthetic) considered necessary by medical professionals.

- I confirm that my child is in good health and I consider him/her fit to participate. I understand the extent and limitations of the insurance cover provided by the school.

- I understand that it is not possible for anyone to guarantee 100% safety, but that the staff leading the party will retain the legal responsibility that they have in law.

Signed.............................................. Date.......................................................

Full name of parent/carer.......................................................................................

Telephone: mobile..................... home............................. work....................

Address.....................................................................................................................

.................................................................................................................................

.................................................................................................................................

# Students' checklist

Students will be curious and possibly anxious about the proposed trip, so it's a good idea to give them the opportunity to ask questions. They will come up with a number of questions of their own, but here are some typical ones:

- Where am I going? What are we going to do there?
- Who is my supervisor? How do I contact them when we are on our trip?
- Are there any dangerous situations that I need to know about? What are the emergency procedures?
- What should I take with me (clothing, equipment)? Do I have to wear uniform? Can I take valuables (eg cameras)?
- What is the code of conduct?
- What is the address and phone number of where we are staying?
- What are the sleeping/washing arrangements?
- What should I do if I am worried or unhappy about anything?

# Evaluation form

After you've completed your visit, take time to reflect on what went well and
what you'd like to improve for future visits.

1 = unsatisfactory     5 = excellent

Food ☐

Accommodation ☐

Travel ☐

Guest teachers ☐

Organisation before the visit ☐

During the visit ☐

After the visit ☐

Quality of information for parents ☐

Quality of information from parents ☐

Dealing with unexpected events ☐

Wet weather contingency, timings ☐

Volunteer supervisors knew what to do ☐

Students' behaviour ☐

Toilet facilities ☐

Tour operator

Support from school colleagues ☐

Relevance of worksheets ☐

Quality of extension activities ☐

Usefulness of school educational visits policy ☐

Overall quality of experience

What I liked most
..............................................................
..............................................................

What I liked least
..............................................................

What I'd do differently
..............................................................
..............................................................

# Pupils' evaluation form

Don't forget to ask your students (and any volunteer supervisors) what they enjoyed most and least about the visit. You might be surprised!

I visited.........................................................

I had been there before/never been there before.

What I liked most about the trip

...........................................................................

What I liked least about the trip

...........................................................................

If 5 is GREAT and 1 is AWFUL, grade the following:

| Travel | 1 2 3 4 5 |
| --- | --- |
| Food | 1 2 3 4 5 |
| Worksheet | 1 2 3 4 5 |
| Site | 1 2 3 4 5 |
| Accommodation | 1 2 3 4 5 |
| Guest teachers | 1 2 3 4 5 |
| Other | 1 2 3 4 5 |

If I could do anything differently, I would

...........................................................................

...........................................................................

# What would you do if...?

The chances are your trip will go smoothly and there won't be any emergencies. But if there are, will you be ready? By planning for the worst and hoping for the best, you should enjoy a safe and successful trip. Take a few minutes to look through this list and think what you would do in each circumstance:

Major delays/strikes; food poisoning (en masse); serious injury or accident; staff/pupil/tour operator being arrested; minor injury; unruly behaviour; losing a pupil; horrible hotels; drivers who get lost (have local maps or GPS!); adverse weather conditions: forest fires/avalanche/flooding; political unrest/demonstrations.

Make your own list specific to the place you are visiting.

**In all situations**
- Do not speak to the media or give out names – appoint a designated media spokesperson from the school (usually the headteacher)
- Don't discuss legal liability except with your headteacher or insurer
- Have a back-up plan if mobile phones don't work

# What to do in a medical emergency

If the worst happened, do you have all the information you need?

- Prior knowledge of area and facilities; phone number/address/contact name
- Awareness of common diseases in certain countries and the main symptoms
- Details of any special medical needs, eg allergy to penicillin
- A named deputy who can step in if you are ill or injured and someone in the UK who can come and help at short notice

Below are listed some typical responses in an emergency:

- Have a qualified first aider with kit: assess situation and safeguard uninjured
- Attend to casualty – choose adult to stay with injured person at all times
- Inform emergency services and anyone else who needs to know (parents, school, embassy/consulate, insurers, tour operator etc)
- Keep a written record and complete an accident report form

# Other emergency situations

**Losing a pupil**
- When did you last see them? Who saw them last?
- Where is the agreed rendezvous point/time?
- Do they have a mobile phone? Do they have their hotel address?
- Call the police with details – note their local phone number

**Being arrested**
- Contact British Embassy/Consulate with details of incident
- Select a member of staff to stay with person arrested
- Contact headteacher, insurers (for legal representation), and parents

**Travel disruption**
- Are there other methods of travel available (with risk assessment)?
- Do you have cash/credit card for transport/hotels (with contact details)?

# Accident report form

**Details of person completing this report**

Name..................................................................

Address (if non-staff volunteer)..............................................    Position................................

Signature.............................................................    Telephone................................

Date................................

**Details of accident/incident**

What happened. Give cause (how and why) if known

When (date and time)................................

Where................................

**Details of any persons injured**

Name (student/staff/volunteer/other)................................

Address................................

Nature of injury................................    Telephone................................

Treatment given................................

Taken to hospital? Yes/No. If yes, which hospital and how taken?................    Administered by................................

Off school as a result of accident/incident? Yes/No. If yes, no. days................................

**For completion by the Health and Safety Officer**

Accident/incident investigated? Yes/No

Written investigation report necessary? Yes/No

Written investigation report completed? Yes/No

RIDDOR reportable? Yes/No. If yes, date reported................................

# Useful publications

*Health and Safety of Pupils on Educational Visits.* DfEE
*Avoiding Ill Health at Open Farms – Advice to teachers AIS23 (Revised).* DfES
*Group Safety at Water Margins.* DfES
*Guidance on First Aid for Schools 1998.* DfEE
*Safety on School Journeys* – NUT and RoSPA (free)
*Safety on British Beaches* – The Royal Life Saving Society and RoSPA
*Safety in Outdoor Activity Centres: Guidance, Circular 22/94* – DfEE Publications
*Streetwise Guide* – Metropolitan Police
*Supporting Students with Medical Needs 1996* – DfEE and Department of Health
*Taking a Minibus Abroad* – DET
*Guides to the Law for School Governors* – DfES (detailed guidance for LEAs and schools on charging for school trips)
*Home from Home 1998* – Central Bureau for Educational Visits and Exchanges
*Making the Most of Your Partner School Abroad 1991* – CBEVE
*Overseas Expeditions* – The Outdoor Education Advisers' Panel
*Everyone's guide to RIDDOR '95 (1996)* – HSE31 – ISBN 0 7176 1077 2
*Reporting school accidents (1997) EDIS 1* – free

# Useful websites

www.dfes.gov.uk/teachers/school_journeys
www.teachernet.gov.uk/management/healthandsafety/visits
www.outdoor-learning.org
www.rospa.co.uk
www.aala.org
www.britishcouncil.org/cbiet
www.isaaa.org.uk
www.hse.gov.uk/pubns
www.radar.org.uk – the disability network
www.riddor.gov.uk – Reporting of Injuries, Diseases and Dangerous Occurrences Regulations

# Where to find places to visit

www.educationalvisitsuk.com

www.schooltrips.co.uk

www.24hourmuseum.org.uk

www.nationaltrust.org.uk

www.englishheritage.org.uk

www.pgl.co.uk –
  activity and adventure holidays

www.theaward.org –
  Duke of Edinburgh Award

www.outwardbound-uk.org –
  the Outward Bound Trust

# Fundraising websites

**www.practicalfunding.org.uk**
**www.tes.co.uk/NQT/noticeboard/index.asp** – list of useful websites
**www.awardsforall.org.uk** – grants from £500 to £2,000
**www.socrates-uk.net** – Comenius grants
**www.Bag2school.com** – buying unwanted clothing
**www.moneytoschools.com** – buying old ink cartridges and other ideas
**www.g-nation.co.uk/teachers** – information on organising fundraising activities
**www.schoolzone.co.uk** or **www.schoolkitty.co.uk** – make products for schools to sell
**www.amazon.co.uk** – set up a link to become an 'Amazon Associate'
**www.free2give.co.uk** – become a 'shopping portal'
**www.icfm.org.uk** – The Institute of Fundraising
**www.charity-fundraising.info** – set up a charity

# About the author

**Jane West**

Before training to be a teacher, Jane West worked for a number of national organisations including three years at the National Gallery in London. Later she gained a Diploma in Marketing and became director of a community centre in London's East End, establishing an after school homework and reading group, a drama and film club and a summer literacy programme. She now works full time as a freelance writer specialising in education, and is editor of Gifted & Talented Update. She has produced teaching and educational visit materials for groups as diverse as The National Trust, Bethnal Green Museum of Childhood and the environmental pressure group Surfers Against Sewage. She writes extensively for the educational press and has also written a number of fiction books for children.

www.janewestwriting.co.uk

# Order Form

### Your details

Name _____

Position _____

School _____

Address _____

_____

_____

Telephone _____

Fax _____

E-mail _____

VAT No. (EC only) _____

Your Order Ref _____

### Please send me:

| | | No. copies |
|---|---|---|
| Trips & Visits | Pocketbook | [ ] |
| _____ | Pocketbook | [ ] |
| _____ | Pocketbook | [ ] |
| _____ | Pocketbook | [ ] |
| _____ | Pocketbook | [ ] |

### Order by Post

## Teachers'
## Pocketbooks

Laurel House, Station Approach
Alresford, Hants. SO24 9JH  UK

**Teachers' Pocketbooks**

### Order by Phone, Fax or Internet

Telephone: +44 (0)1962 735573
Facsimile:  +44 (0)1962 733637
E-mail: sales@teacherspocketbooks.co.uk
Web: www.teacherspocketbooks.co.uk